Witches

American adaptation by Pat Arthur

Library of Congress Catalog Number: 81-81307
ISBN: 0-675-01090-X
Published by
TRADE DIVISION
Charles E. Merrill Publishing Company
A Bell & Howell Company
1300 Alum Creek Drive
Columbus, Ohio 43216

Witches

by
Colin Hawkins and
an old witch

Pointed hat ⟶

Rare Black Ferret,
very powerful
charm against
pickpockets.
↓

Raven

Long black gown

Carriage for carrying

Which is Witch?

According to ancient writings,

"A witch be known by her great age, wrinkled face, furrowed brow, hairy lip, goober teeth, squint eye, squeaking voice, scolding tongue, ragged coat, and the cat or dog by her side."

Well, when you think about it, this could be a description of lots of people. You see, throughout the centuries many have mistakenly feared witches. The stories of a witch changing you into a cat or a toadstool or a bat or even, if you are a prince, into a frog, have been greatly exaggerated.

Now there is no doubt that some witches have a nastier side to their magic, a little bit of mischief here, a little bit of hocum there. But on the whole, witches have usually practiced their arts to good purpose. The truth is, many witches have grown old before their time, worn out by the toil and trouble of slaving over a hot cauldron, just trying to help ordinary people.

If you are one who's never heard the truth about witches, about the goodness of their powers and practices, then this book is for you. And once you've learned almost all there is to know about witches, don't be surprised if you find that some of your favorite people share many of the same charms.

Very wise familiar

Familiar atop a famil

A familiar hat

A furry familiar

A familiar smile

Suspended familiar

A familiar pair

Spotted familiar

Looks Familiar

That familiar-looking cat around the corner may not be a real cat
at all. It could be a witch's familiar, a small witch helper
that has taken the form of a cat. Familiars are used by witches
to gather information and gossip. They take messages to other
witches. They help to gather ingredients for spells and generally
make themselves useful.

Not all familiars are cats, of course. They can be dogs, birds, toads,
crocodiles, and even bugs, but cats are most popular because they
can forecast the weather and help a witch to change it. When a
witch's cat claws at the carpet or at the curtains, it is raising the
wind. If it washes its ears or sneezes, it is bringing rain.

Though familiars are a great help to a witch and good company, they
often become too familiar. Cats will often walk all over their witch.
The expression "familiarity breeds contempt" comes from this habit.

"Watch the birdie".

An over
familiar
familiar.

Ravens sitting on the roof will bring good luck to the household.

Weather vanes are a protection against the powers of darkness.

To be near a witch elm tree after dusk is to run the risk of being placed in the power of witches.

Multiple cat doors

Broom garden

Home Sour Home

Witches tend to live in houses of great age, but it is not always easy to tell a witch's house for certain. Signs to look for are an unlucky number on the door, a very slender garage, multiple cat entrances, blackened windows, a weather vane blowing backwards, a witch answering the door.

Inside, a witch's house is nicely decorated with cat hair carpet, raven flock wallpaper, and cobweb curtains at the windows. Upstairs, the bedrooms contain beds, baskets, bees' nests, perches, crocodile cots, and cats' cradles.

You will notice that witches never have newspapers delivered to their homes. The stale news of a daily paper is of no interest to them. They prefer to read the future in the flames of the fire. Books are another matter. A witch needs a good library of recipe books and spellbooks, and notebooks for writing up new spells.

A witch's library will often contain an assortment of bookworms, book bugs, book caterpillars, or even the odd book frog hopping along the shelves.

odd book frog

book caterpillar

bookworm

book bugs

Bats hate water.

Baths are rarely if ever, a private affair.

Soapwort bubble bath

A water-lovin familia

Hot-footed Kettle

A familiar cat scrubbing a familiar back.

Hubble Bubble Bath

Contrary to popular belief, witches like to shower or bathe every day, and most wash and curl their hair at least once a week. Bubbles are a must. Powdered soapwort leaves sprinkled under the faucet produce a luxurious foam in minutes. To create an especially soothing bath after a hectic night, many witches add lavender to the water, a favorite witch scent.

Bath time is also beauty time with extra care given to hair and complexion. Secret health and beauty recipes are handed down from witch mother to witch daughter. Ointments, herbs, lotions, shampoos, powders, and scents, all combine to create the characteristically sleek shiny locks and soft downy skin of a young witch.

Familiars can be a great help at bath time, but water-loving familiars can become a nuisance, particularly in a small tub.

lice hate water, too!

Witch Tip:
Bath water thrown over weeds will encourage hardy growth and a sweet smell.

The normal height of a witch is between 4 feet 6 inches and 8 feet (including hat).

Hat brim can be folded down and tied over the ears in cold weather.

Portable cauldron

Open-finger mittens

Secret pockets

Sturdy leather boots

Night Light Hat complete with funnel and snuffer, used for reading in bed and on moonless nights.

Black thermal undershirt

Eight-button camisole

Winter-weight bloomers.

Black stretch stockings

Witch Wear

Witches are old-fashioned in their choice of clothes. They believe that their garments should be durable and a good value for their money. Clothes should be warm for chilly October flights and reasonably waterproof, especially during June rain bottling. They need to be a color that will not show cauldron stains or garden grime.

It is important that witch's clothes be comfortable, allowing complete freedom of movement for arm-waving and leg-jerking spells. The classic witch gown has extra-deep pockets for keeping such witch essentials as sandwiches, tea flasks, safety pins, string, old stockings, and toads.

A Witch's Bag
and some of its contents.

Snap purse

pocket spell book
or pocket
spells.

Flying ointment

Whistle for calling up the wind and police dogs.

Witch hat pin
(a must for flying).

Small umbrella for small showers and squalls.

Snap Cackle Pop

A prune a day keeps th' witch doctor away.

A breakfast of ant eggs, eat raw, will rest the senses.

Pains in the belly can be cure' with jelly.

Bats will rarely, if ever, get up in time for breakfast.

Second
helpings

Dropping
in for
breakfast

Toasted
cheese,
please.

Witches eat heartily at breakfast. Most are especially fond of witch's porridge, made from preserved frogspawn. A favorite second course is dawn-gathered toadstools on toast. After that, for the sour-toothed, there is delicious lemon juice jam with acorn bread and steaming hot dandelion coffee. In the old days, witches had to cast a spell to sour their milk, but nowadays sour cream can be easily found at the supermarket.

Not so with food for the familiars; very few shops stock canned frog food, raven seed, batburgers, or choice cuts for crocodiles.   So breakfast can take a long time, even with an imaginative witch at the stove. And with so many to feed, it's not surprising that the cupboard is often bare.

A cat on the mat
is a cat that is
fat.

And when the cupboard is bare...

The spell to make the bus come.

Note use of thumb.

Shock in Store

Sometimes this spell can be too strong.

Whistling up sausages

Only the stalest bread will do for a really fussy witch.

French bread should be wrapped before leaving the bakery.

Year candle

Candlestick maker

Since the invention of electricity, witches have been quite welcome at the candlestick maker's shop.

In times gone by, a witch had to trail from shop to shop for her provisions. Today she can shop in half the time and with twice the fun. The supermarket has become a great place for witches to meet, exchange gossip, news, and the latest spells, and to take part in the weekly race to the check-out line. It is worth noting that witches like to shop between 5:30 and 7:00 p.m. on Friday evenings—a time to avoid supermarkets unless, that is, you enjoy dodging speeding grocery carts.

Green Fingers

Few shops stock the variety of ingredients that a witch needs constantly at hand for her spells. So a witch must cultivate her own garden, keeping the ground free from flowers that choke the weeds and clearing mushrooms from space where nettles and toadstools could grow.

Because witches can hear a plant in pain, they are careful to cast plant sleeping spells before cutting a single stem. No crying creepers, shrieking violets, mournful moss, or wisteria with hysteria will be found in a witch's garden. Nor will you find plants tied to stakes or forced to stand in rows against the wall.

Favorite witch plants are nettles, dandelions, the tastier toadstools, skunk cabbage, chickweed, thistles, rosemary, foxgloves, cucumbers, and roses.

Hollyhocks: a good remedy for spongy gums.

A salve of skunk cabbage and petals of rose, Will soothe the pain of a scrape on the n

A scarecrow

unscared crows

To stay in fine
fettle,
eat a
nettle.

Chickweed
A cure for itch.

andelions
ll induce restful
sleep rarely.

Not much room
for mushrooms.

A mouse dipped twice in a cauldron of foxglove and boar grease guarantees an excellent flying ointment... and bathes the mouse in the bargain.

It is thought that there are more witch cures for warts than there are warts in the world.

The dust from a moth in the broth will cure cough.

Witch magic po best when is done in

Spelling Lessons

Witches are often called out at night to cast spells or perform a bit of hocus pocus. Because a witch must be well rested to make potions that work, they have to learn to snatch what sleep they can, snoozing in an easy chair or dozing in front of the television.

To make an active potion, the witch needs not only the right mixture, cooked at the exact temperature, but she also needs to know the precise form of words for casting the spell.

A young witch must practice for hours after school. She must take cooking lessons, study recipes, learn shorthand and typing and millions of chants, calls, shrieks, mutters, and incantations. Without a good background in spelling, a witch cannot hope for a successful career.

The simplest spells deal with the weather. To raise a storm at sea, for instance, a witch merely has to swing a fish three times round her head and then throw it into the sea, chanting

"Screech, screech, screech some more,
Make the sea rage and roar."

More difficult but more worthwhile are spells for curing ailments.

Successful rainmaking witch   Dry toad

Curious Cures

If you have warts, try these cures. Place in a bag as many pebbles as you have warts and leave the bag at a crossroads. The warts will be transferred to whomever picks up the bag. Or, stick a pin into an ash tree, reciting

"Ashen tree, ashen tree,
Take these warts away from me."

Rainwater collected and bottled in June will cure eye disorders.

As a cure for toothache a mole should be worn around the neck.

For a tummy ache, stand on
your head for two minutes and say
   "Ickle, dickle, dockle day,
   Take this horrid pain away."

For a cough, stay in bed
and take thistle soup three
times a day.

For headaches, close your eyes,
stay very still, and count silently
to a hundred. This cure may
have to be tried over and
over again before it works.

For a fever, take a pinch of
compressed spiders' webs in
juice before breakfast.

For sore knees, boil up
some cabbage and cucumbers
with some chocolate sponge,
and eat the mixture at bedtime.

For a runny nose, hold your
ears and touch your toes.

For finger warts, tie a bow
on the finger with the wart.
Then standing on tiptoes,
sprinkle chickweed powder
on a resting dog.
Repeat every night
for a week.

Sore feet

Greasy boars are
not easy to find
and so should
be allowed
to drive
the chair
occasionally.

A witch with
sore feet can't fly.

Witches have yet to discover a lasting
cure for sore feet. However, a ride
with a greasy bore has long been
thought to have some beneficial effect.

Another wart cure

Reading the leaves

Devil's food cake

Let the tea stand.

Burdock nectar

Black olives in syrup

Red newt jelly

Mule muffins

Cold cross buns

Dandelion mousse

May Day tarts

Goa

L ice

Witch Delights

Witches like to get together. Morning coffee gatherings, drives, coach outings, tennis tournaments, and tea parties are all good excuses for cozy gossip. For entertainment after a tea party, witches like to watch television or tell each other's fortune in the tea leaves (witches never use tea bags). After drinking the tea, each witch passes her cup to the left. The witch next to her swirls it three times in her left hand before draining off the dregs. Patterns near the handle represent the near future, those in the upper part more distant events, and those in the bottom the very distant future. Patterns shaped like triangles, spades, clubs, snakes, fish, or crabs spell bad luck; moonshapes, clover leaves, flowers, trees, crows, and the number seven foretell good luck.

After a supper party, witches like to dance, practicing the latest steps and listening to the top ten.

A witched kettle never boils.

Dandelion juice

A slow kettle could be bewitched and contain a toad.

A flight
or
cackle
of
witches

Flying High

Goats can be flown if no other choice is available.

Ancient stories tell of witches flying in the sky, screeching and cackling. But in truth, broomstick flying is dangerous, cold, and uncomfortable, so most witches prefer to travel by bus, bike, or car. Witches usually only fly to important gatherings such as conventions or Halloween. But in cases of public transportation strikes or great emergency, the art of flying comes in handy.

When witches do fly, they usually use broomsticks, though sometimes they use cats, roosters, horses, large dogs, or if really desperate, goats. A horse found in the morning, tired, sweating, and not fit for work might well have been hag-ridden during the night.

Riding to a witch convention

Before takeoff, a witch must rub flying ointment all over her body. The smell of this mixture of mouse-dipped foxglove juice and boar's grease is a sure sign that a witch will be flying tonight.

Shape-changing into a bird, fly, or other flying creature is a short cut to flying. Witches can change themselves into any creature they wish, from ants to weasels, though cats and rabbits are the most popular choices. A witch is usually unable to change into a dove.

Shape Shifting
Cats and rabbits are the most popular form taken, and occasionally flies.

Shape-changing into doves was never successful.

High Jinks

The witches' year begins at Halloween, a time when ghosts, goblins, young witches, and children roam around demanding treats or offering tricks. Jack-o-lanterns of every kind cast eerie lights to welcome these little trick-or-treaters with their bags.

Dancing the traditional May Day Dance around the maypole.

To dance the Widdershins (the dance of the witches), form a circle 13 feet in diameter around a bonfire, and dance in the opposite direction to that of the sun's path around the sky.

On Halloween, adult witches gather
at midnight and dance around the
flames until dawn. Round and round
the bonfire, dancing widdershins,
waltzing, quickstepping, two-stepping,
slowstepping, sidestepping, twisting,
shaking, and just doing their thing.
No other festival lives up to Halloween
for fashions, flying, and fun.

New Year's, for instance, is a time for
cleanliness and goodliness. Witches burn
candles as a sign of their purity.

On Valentine's Day, young witches place
bay leaves under their pillows in order to
dream of their future husbands. It is not
known how accurate their dreams are.

May Day celebrates the start of summer
and is time for more high jinks. Young
witches dance round the maypole,
hoping to attract enough attention to be
chosen Queen of May.

If a young witch has not found a
husband by May Day, she can try again
around the Midsummer's Eve bonfire.

At the harvest festival of Midsummer's
Eve, young witches often bake magic
cakes with the newly harvested corn
to offer to their sweethearts. If they
cannot charm a man with their charms,
they will charm him with their spells.

Some needed more purification than others.

With bay leaves under her pillow, a girl will dream of her future husband.

The first cake of Midsummer's Eve

Witches enjoy playing the ancient game of pass the toad.

Witch Facts?

A favorite spell of witches and wizards is to turn a Prince into a frog, or Rover into a toad.

If you want to know the way ask an old witch.

Witches have been known to live to a great age, some well beyond 300 years.

An old witch in her later years will teach all she knows to a young novice witch.

…any witches possess great skill …the art of …stick …ing.

…best …chosen for the Witch Olympics.

In ancient times both male and female witches were often said to have the ability to worry sheep.

Two worried sheep

another worried sheep

Misunderstood black cat →

Witches are very fond of cats, specially black cats. They are the most popular choice as familiars and, like witches, have …ong been misunderstood.

Twins, particularly witch twins, have long been thought to possess unique powers and have been mistakenly regarded by many to be double trouble.

One thing more...

If you should meet a witch some day,
be very kind because, like everyone else,
witches need lots of love.